Contents

The Wind in the Willows

KENNETH GRAHAME

Level 2

Retold by Anne Collins
Series Editors: Andy Hopkins and Jocelyn Potter

Pearson Education Limited
Edinburgh Gate, Harlow,
Essex CM20 2JE, England
and Associated Companies throughout the world.

ISBN 0 582 42660 X

This edition first published 2000

NEW EDITION

Typeset by Pantek Arts Ltd, Maidstone, Kent
Set in 11/14pt Bembo
Printed in Denmark by Nørhaven A/S, Viborg

Published by Pearson Education Limited in association with
Penguin Books Ltd, both companies being subsidiaries of Pearson Plc

For a complete list of the titles available in the Penguin Readers series please write to your local
Pearson Education office or to: Marketing Department, Penguin Longman Publishing,
5 Bentinck Street, London W1M 5RN.

Introduction

'Sit down there, Toad,' said Badger kindly. Then he turned to Rat and Mole and said, 'Toad's going to stop driving cars.'

But Toad smiled and said, 'No, no, no, I love cars. They're the most wonderful things in the world. I'm not going to stop driving.'

Toad is a dangerous driver. He has six accidents, and the police are very angry with him. But then Toad buys another car. His friends – Rat, Mole and Badger – have to stop him driving. But can they stop him? Or will Toad go to prison?

The Wind in the Willows (1908) is Kenneth Grahame's best and most famous book. The four animals in the story are good friends, but they are very different. Badger doesn't like visitors. Rat is strong and brave and loves the river. Mole is afraid of things. Toad is always looking for exciting new adventures.

Kenneth Grahame was born in Edinburgh, Scotland, in 1859. He went to school in Oxford, and later he worked in the Bank of England. He wasn't always happy at the bank, but he did very well there. He had a very important job, and his name was on the banknotes. He left the bank in 1907 and died in 1932.

Kenneth Grahame loved children, small wild animals and life in the country. When he could get away from London, he went for walks in the country. There he wrote stories. Before *The Wind in the Willows*, he wrote two books for and about children: *The Golden Age* (1895) and *Dream Days* (1898). *The Wind in the Willows* is a wonderful book. People of all ages enjoy and remember it.

Animals in this Story

weasel

otter

mole

water rat

toad

badger

Chapter 1   The River Bank

Mole worked hard all morning in his house under the ground. It was spring and he wanted to clean his house after the winter. There was a lot of work for him.

Suddenly he felt tired and wanted to stop. So he climbed up his tunnel – up! up! – to the ground. Then he jumped out of his hole and started walking. He liked being outside. Mole felt very happy.

He walked for a long time. Then suddenly he saw something new. It was a river. It looked beautiful with the sun on it. Mole stood and watched it for a long time. Then he sat down on the bank.

He saw a dark hole in the other bank across the river. Then he saw two brown eyes inside the hole. The eyes moved and a head came out: it was the Water Rat.

'Hello, Mole!' said Rat.

'Hello, Rat!' said Mole.

'Would you like to come over here?' Rat asked next.

'Yes – but can I?' said Mole. He didn't know very much about the river or boats.

'Of course you can!' laughed Rat. 'I'll come for you in my boat.' There was a little blue and white boat outside his hole. Rat got into it and came across the river.

Mole was afraid when he first got into the boat. But he was also excited. 'This is a wonderful day!' he told Rat. 'It's my first time in a boat!'

'Really? First time in a boat?' said Rat. He was very surprised. 'But boats are very nice. Listen, Mole, are you doing anything this morning? Let's go out in the boat. We can take some food and go out on the river all day.'

1

'Oh, Rat!' said Mole. 'This is the best day of my life!'

'Wait a minute, then. I'll go and get some food,' said Rat, and he climbed into his hole. Two minutes later he came back. He had a very large box with him. 'Here, Mole. Put this under your feet.'

Rat started to row. Mole sat back and looked at everything. It was beautiful: the sun on the water, the green banks of the river and the noise of the water on the bottom of the boat.

Mole and Rat didn't speak for a long time. Then Mole said quietly, 'So you live by the river, Rat – that's a great life!'

'By it, with it, on it and in it,' said Rat. 'The river is my brother and sister, my mother and father, my friend, my food and drink – and, of course, I can wash in it. It's my world.'

The Mole saw a lot of dark trees. 'What's that place there, Ratty?' he asked.

'Oh, that,' said Rat. 'That's the Wild Wood. We don't go there often.'

'Why?' asked Mole. 'Aren't the animals in the Wild Wood very nice?'

'Some of them aren't bad,' said Rat slowly. 'Badger lives there and he's a good friend. But the weasels live there too – I don't know them very well, but ...' He stopped. Mole didn't ask any more questions about the Wild Wood.

Later, Rat stopped the boat in a quiet place and said, 'Here's a good place for lunch.'

He helped Mole out of the boat on to the bank. Then he got out the box of food. 'Let's eat, Mole. Are you hungry?'

Mole was very hungry. They had a wonderful lunch and then they sat on the bank in the sun.

'Rat,' said Mole. 'I think there's something in the water there, but I can't really see it.'

Suddenly, there was a nose above the water. It was Otter.

'Here, Mole. Put this under your feet.'

'Why didn't you ask me to lunch, Ratty?' he cried, when he saw the food box.

'I didn't have time,' said Rat. 'Oh, Otter, this is my friend, Mr Mole.'

'How do you do, Mole,' said Otter.

'How do you do, Otter,' said Mole.

'This is a beautiful day,' said Otter. 'Everybody's out on the river. Toad's out. He's got a new boat, new clothes – everything's new.' Otter looked at Rat and they laughed.

'Toad's very nice,' said Rat, 'but he always has new ideas.'

A short time later, Otter said, 'I have to go now.'

'We have to go too, Mole,' said Rat.

'Can I row, please?' asked Mole, when they were in the boat.

'No, Mole, not today. It isn't easy.'

So Mole sat down. But after half an hour he tried again. This time he didn't say anything. He got up and pushed Rat out of the way. Then he started to row.

'Stop it! Don't be stupid!' shouted Rat. 'You can't row!'

But it was too late. The boat turned over and Rat and Mole were in the water.

'Help!' thought Mole. He went down and down. 'It's very cold! Perhaps I'm going to die!' But Rat could swim very well. He pushed Mole up and then pushed him to the bank. Mole was very wet and cold and unhappy.

'Stand up, Mole,' said Rat. 'Run up and down the bank. It will make you dry again. I'm going to get the boat.'

Rat rowed home.

'Sorry, Ratty,' Mole said. 'I was very stupid. I won't do it again.'

'It's not a problem,' Rat answered. 'A little water is nothing to a Water Rat. But, Mole, why don't you come and stay with me by the river? Then I can teach you to row and swim.'

'Oh, Rat, thank you,' said Mole. 'I'd really like that.' He felt very happy.

'Why didn't you ask me to lunch, Ratty?'

And so Mole stayed at Rat's house. They had many happy days by the river, on the river and in the river. Mole learned to swim and to row. And he learned to love the river.

Chapter 2   Mole Meets Toad

One warm summer morning, Rat and Mole sat on the river bank.

'Ratty,' said Mole. 'Can we visit Toad? You told me a lot of things about him. I'd like to meet him.'

'Of course, Mole,' answered Rat. 'Get the boat out and we'll go now. Toad likes visitors. He'll be very happy when he sees us.'

'Is Toad nice?' asked Mole when they were in the boat.

'Yes, he is – very nice. Not very clever, perhaps, and sometimes he talks too much, but he's a good Toad.'

A short time later, they saw Toad Hall from the river. It was a big, old house with a beautiful garden. Toad had many fine boats. They left their little boat with Toad's boats.

'Let's go and find Toad,' said Rat.

They found Toad in the garden. He jumped up when he saw them.

'Ratty! I wanted to see you and here you are,' he cried.

'Toad, this is my friend, Mole,' said Rat. 'Let's sit quietly for a minute. Isn't this a beautiful place, Mole?'

Before Mole could answer, Toad cried, 'Yes, it's the finest house on the river – or anywhere!'

Mole looked at Rat and laughed. Toad saw this and his face turned red.

'I know I always talk about my house, Ratty. But it *is* a nice house. Now, I want you to help me.'

'Is it about your boats?' asked Rat.

'Oh, no!' said Toad. 'Boats are boring. I've got a new idea – something better than boats. Come with me and I'll show you.' He took Rat and Mole to the back of the house.

A short time later, they saw Toad Hall from the river.

'There!' he said. 'That's my new life!' He showed them a beautiful red and yellow caravan. 'I'm going to go everywhere in that caravan. I'll go to a new place every day. Come inside and see! Everything is there.'

Rat didn't want to go inside the caravan, but Mole was very excited. Toad showed him everything – the kitchen, the little beds, the books, the games, the food. 'I've got everything,' he said. 'When we start this afternoon, you'll see.'

'Toad,' said Rat slowly. 'Did you say "we" and "start" and "this afternoon"? Because I'm not leaving my river and my house and my boat. I'm not going anywhere. And Mole doesn't want to go. . .'

'No, no, I don't,' said Mole quietly. But he really wanted to go. He was in love with the little red and yellow caravan.

Rat didn't want to hurt his friend, so he said, 'Shall we think about it?'

'Yes,' said Toad. 'Let's think about it at lunch. You *will* stay for lunch?'

At lunch, Toad talked about his plans, and Mole got more and more excited about the caravan. In the end, Rat said, 'Toad, we'll come with you. But only for a short journey. Only a day or two.'

Chapter 3   The Open Road

So the three friends left Toad Hall that afternoon. The weather was lovely – warm sun, but not too hot. They went a long way in the caravan and saw a lot of new things. Late in the evening they stopped and ate. Toad talked about his plans for the next day.

'This is a good life!' he said happily. 'This is better than your river, Rat!'

'No, it isn't,' said Rat sadly.

He showed them a beautiful red and yellow caravan.

'Ratty,' said Mole very quietly because he didn't want Toad to hear. 'Do you want to go home? We can leave very early in the morning.'

'No, no,' answered Rat. 'Thank you, Mole, but we can't leave Toad. We have to stay with him. He'll only be interested in the caravan for a short time. Then he'll find something new.'

The next morning, Rat and Mole got up early, but they couldn't wake Toad up. And so they washed the cups and plates and cooked the breakfast. Then they gave the horse some food. There was a lot of work. They worked, but Toad slept. After they finished, he woke up.

They had another fine day outside. But on the second evening, Mole and Rat told Toad, 'You have to help us with the work.' Toad didn't like helping very much.

The next day, they were on a quiet road when something happened. Mole was in front with the horse, and Rat and Toad walked behind the caravan. Toad talked and talked. Suddenly, in front of them, they saw a lot of dust. This dust moved very fast. There was a loud noise too: ' *Poop, poop !*'

Then the dust and the noise were on top of the animals. They couldn't see in the dust and they couldn't think. The noise was too loud. What was this thing? They tried to jump out of its way but they couldn't.

The thing went past them in a minute. Slowly the dust went away and the three animals could see again. The old horse was very afraid and wanted to run away. It pulled the caravan, and the caravan fell over in the road. The windows and many things inside were broken.

Rat was very angry. He jumped up and down in the middle of the road and shouted angrily. But Toad wasn't angry. He sat in the road and looked very happy. He said again and again, *'Poop, poop !'*

Rat was very surprised. He thought, 'What's wrong with Toad? Why isn't he angry?'

There was a loud noise too: 'Poop poop!'

'Come here, Toad,' he said. 'Help us with the caravan. Let's try and move it.' But Toad didn't move.

'So that's a car!' he said quietly. 'Wasn't it wonderful! Wasn't it exciting? That's the only thing for me now.'

'What shall we do, Rat?' asked Mole. 'The caravan is broken. Toad, you'll have to go to the police station. Tell the police about that car.'

'Police station?' said Toad. 'Why? I don't want to tell the police anything. I never want to see this caravan, or hear about it, again. Caravans are boring. But cars are wonderful – the most wonderful things in the world.'

'Let's take Toad back to Toad Hall,' said Rat. 'We'll take the horse and walk to the next town. Then we can catch a train home.'

And so Mole and Rat took Toad to Toad Hall. Then they went back to Rat's house by the river. It was very late when they got there. They were very tired. But Rat was happy because he was at home again.

The next day, Toad caught an early train to London. There he bought a large and very expensive car!

Chapter 4   The Wild Wood

Mole wanted to meet Rat's friend, Badger. Badger lived in the Wild Wood. One day Mole said to Rat, 'Let's ask Badger to dinner. Then I can meet him.'

'No, I don't think that's a good idea,' answered Rat. 'Badger doesn't like dinner parties.'

'Can we go and visit him?' asked Mole.

'No, Mole, we can't. We have to wait. Badger will come and visit us in the end. You'll see.' So Mole didn't ask about Badger again.

The summer ended quickly. Rat and Mole were very busy on the river every day. Then winter came. Rat and Mole slept and slept. They got up late and went to bed early. On these short days, Rat sometimes wrote little stories, but usually he only sat by the fire.

Mole began to think about Badger again. One afternoon in the middle of winter, Rat was asleep by the fire. So Mole went out for a walk.

'I think I'll visit Mr Badger,' he thought.

The country was very different in winter. Everything looked dead. The trees weren't green now and the ground was brown. It was very cold so Mole walked quickly. He arrived at the Wild Wood.

Mole went into the wood, and everything got darker and darker. Mole began to see strange faces round him and to hear strange noises. He walked faster and faster. In the wood, day turned into night. Mole was very afraid. The wood got darker again and there were more strange noises. Mole couldn't find his way. He walked and walked. Then he stopped and found a hole under a big tree.

'I can't walk now,' he thought. 'I'm too tired and cold and afraid. I'll wait here for a short time.'

◆

Rat slept for a long time by his fire. When he woke up, he was hungry and thirsty. 'It's tea time,' he thought. 'Mole, shall we have some tea?' he shouted.

But there was no answer. Rat looked for Mole in every room of the house but he couldn't find him. Then he looked in the hall. Mole's coat and winter shoes weren't there.

'So Mole is outside,' thought Rat. 'But why did he go for a walk in winter? Where did he go?' He stopped. 'Oh, no! Perhaps he went to the Wild Wood!'

Rat opened his front door and looked out. Then he went to a cupboard and took out a small gun and a heavy stick.

Mole went into the wood, and everything got darker and darker.

'I'll follow Mole and find him. He doesn't know the Wild Wood and he'll be very afraid!' Rat thought.

It was dark when Rat left home. He walked very quickly to the Wild Wood. When he arrived there, he didn't stop for a minute. He went inside, and called, 'Mole, Mole! Where are you? It's me – Rat!'

He walked for more than an hour, but he couldn't find Mole anywhere. Rat began to be afraid.

'Where is Mole?' he thought. 'Perhaps I'll never see him again.'

Then suddenly, he heard Mole. 'Ratty, is that really you?'

'Mole, where are you?' Rat cried.

'I'm here in this hole under the big tree,' Mole cried.

Rat found the hole and went inside.

'Oh, Rat,' cried Mole. 'I'm very happy now! I was afraid.'

'I'm here now,' said Rat. 'But why did you come here? You were very stupid. The Wild Wood is a bad place. But don't be afraid now. Let's go home.'

'Oh, Ratty,' said Mole. 'I'm very very tired. Please can I sleep first?'

'Of course, Mole,' said Rat kindly.

So Mole slept, and Rat sat and waited. After an hour, Mole woke up. But when they went out of the hole, everywhere looked different. Everything was white.

'It's snow,' said Rat. 'The snow came when you were asleep. Let's go, Mole. We have to get home. But now it's difficult because everything looks different in the snow.'

The two animals walked and walked. But they couldn't find their way out of the Wild Wood. They walked for two hours and they were very tired.

Suddenly, Mole cried, 'Oh, my leg! My leg!'

'What happened?' asked Rat. 'Oh, there's a big cut on your leg. Sit down for a minute, Mole, and I'll look at it. But what did you cut it on?'

Mole sat down in the snow and Rat cleaned the cut. Then he saw something very hard in the ground.

'Look, Mole,' he said. 'You clean your shoes on that. So that means ... there's a house near here.' And he started to look in the snow.

'What *is* Rat thinking about?' Mole thought, but he didn't say anything.

After about ten minutes, Rat cried, 'What did I tell you, Mole? Come and see!' And Rat showed Mole a little door. On the door were the words MR BADGER.

'Ratty,' cried Mole. 'Now I understand. You *are* clever! Is this really Badger's house?'

'Yes,' said Rat. 'We'll be fine now.' He began to hit the door with his hands. He shouted, 'Badger!'

Chapter 5   Mr Badger

After a long time, Rat and Mole heard noises from inside the house. The door opened and somebody shouted angrily,

'Who's there? I don't want any visitors. It's very late.'

'Oh, please can we come in, Badger,' said Rat. 'It's me, Rat, and my friend, Mole. We lost our way in the snow.'

'Ratty, my dear friend,' said Badger. He was friendly now. 'Come inside! And you too, Mole,' he said warmly.

Rat and Mole were happy now. They were out of the Wild Wood. The door closed behind them.

Badger's house was under the ground. He took the two cold animals into his kitchen. There was a big open fire with chairs in front of it. In the middle of the room was a big table, and on the table there was some food. Everything was warm and friendly. It was very different from the snow outside!

Rat and Mole took off their wet coats and shoes, and sat down by the fire. Then Badger cooked a hot dinner for them. They ate and ate. For a long time nobody spoke. Then Rat told Badger their story. After Rat finished, Badger only said, 'You're here now. I'm very happy about that.'

'Badger is a good friend,' Mole thought.

Then Badger wanted to know about life on the river.

'How's Toad?' he asked.

'Things are very bad,' Rat answered sadly. 'His car ran into a tree again last week. We want him to have a driver. But no, Toad wants to drive. He likes driving, but he's really a very dangerous driver.

'Now he's got a new car. It's number seven! He had accidents in the other six cars and the police are very angry with him. But he doesn't want to stop. We have to do something, Badger. We're his friends. He has to stop driving.'

'We can't do anything now,' said Badger. 'It's the middle of winter. But in the summer, when the days are longer – then we'll do something. But now, my friends, it's bedtime. You're very tired.'

Badger showed Mole and Rat their beds, and said, 'Don't get up early in the morning. You can have breakfast later.'

The next morning, Rat and Mole slept and slept. When they got up, they went into the kitchen. There they saw Otter.

'Good morning!' he shouted. 'What are you doing here in the Wild Wood with Badger?'

So Rat and Mole told their story again. When he remembered that day in the dark wood, Mole was very afraid.

'Did you come through the Wild Wood, Otter?' he asked. 'Were you afraid?'

'Me?' cried Otter. 'Afraid? I'm not afraid of anybody or anything. Can I have some breakfast, too? I'm very hungry.'

Rat and Otter were good friends. They talked for a long time about the river. Then after breakfast Badger showed Mole his house. Mole was surprised because Badger's house was very big. He liked it very much.

'My house is under the ground, too,' Mole said. 'I like houses under the ground. They're nice and warm.'

'Yes,' said Badger. 'Do you like Toad's house, Toad Hall? I don't. It's a beautiful house, but it's cold in winter. Down here in my house, summer and winter are the same.'

When they were in the kitchen again, Rat said, 'Let's go home now, Mole. We don't want to be in the Wild Wood again tonight.'

'Don't be afraid,' said Otter. 'I'm coming with you.'

'I know a very good way,' said Badger. 'My house goes a long way under the ground. Come with me and I'll show you. You don't have to go through the Wild Wood.'

Badger took the three animals down many dark tunnels. After a long time, the tunnels ended and they were outside again. But they weren't in the Wild Wood – it was behind them. In front of them they could see the river bank.

'Thank you for everything, Badger,' they said.

A short time later, they arrived at Rat's house. Rat and Mole were very happy. They were at home again.

Chapter 6   Mr Toad

The winter ended. Spring came, and Rat and Mole began their busy life again.

One morning, Badger visited Rat and Mole.

'Badger!' cried Rat. 'This is nice! Come and have some breakfast!'

'Hello, Rat,' Badger said quietly. 'No, I won't have any breakfast, thank you. I'm here because it's time.'

In front of them they could see the river bank.

'What time?' asked Rat.

'We have to talk to Toad,' Badger answered. 'He's got another new car. I want you and Mole to come to Toad Hall with me.'

'Yes, of course, Badger,' Rat said. 'Let's go there now.'

When the three friends arrived at Toad Hall, they saw Toad's new car. It was big and red. Then Toad came out of his house. His clothes were new too.

'Good morning, everybody!' he cried when he saw them. 'Are you coming in my beautiful new ... er ... er...' Then Toad saw Badger's face and stopped. What was wrong?

'Take him inside the house,' Badger said to Rat and Mole. Then he said to Toad, 'You're not going anywhere in that car. So you can take off those stupid clothes.'

'No,' said Toad. 'What do you mean, Badger? This is my house and my car. I can go out when I want to go out.'

'Listen, Toad,' said Badger. 'The police are very angry with you. You're a very dangerous driver. You have to stop driving. I want to talk to you.' And Badger took Toad into another room and closed the door.

After an hour, the door opened and the two animals came out. Toad looked very unhappy.

'Sit down there, Toad,' said Badger kindly. Then he turned to Rat and Mole and said, 'Toad's going to stop driving cars.'

But Toad smiled and said, 'No, no, no, I love cars. They're the most wonderful things in the world. I'm not going to stop driving.'

'What?' cried Badger. He was very surprised. 'You are a bad animal, Toad. Mole, Rat, take Toad to his bedroom. Lock the door and come back here.'

Toad was very, very angry. He fought hard, but Mole and Rat took him to his bedroom. They locked him inside.

When they came back, Badger said, 'Toad is very angry. We'll have to stay with him and talk to him again.'

Then Toad came out of his house.

And so Badger, Rat and Mole stayed with Toad. One of them slept in Toad's room at night. Toad shouted and cried. He threw things round the room. Then he was quieter.

One morning, Rat went into Toad's room. Toad was in bed. He looked very quiet and sad.

'How are you today, Toad?' asked Rat.

Toad didn't answer. Then he said quietly, 'I don't feel very well, dear Ratty. I'm a bad Toad. I know I'm a bad driver. But I feel very ill. Perhaps I'm going to die. Then your work will end.'

'What are you talking about, Toad?' said Rat. 'Get out of bed. Let's play a game or something.'

'Oh, Ratty, I can't. I'll never play games again,' said Toad. He stopped for a minute and then said, 'I want the doctor, Ratty. Can you bring him to me, please?'

Rat began to be afraid. Was Toad really very ill?

'Yes, Toad, of course,' he said. 'I'll get the doctor.' He ran out of the room. He didn't lock the door.

Toad jumped out of bed. He wasn't really ill! He sang a little song and then he dressed. Toad went quietly out of the room and left the house. Nobody saw him.

Badger and Mole were very angry with Rat.

'Now we'll have to stay at Toad Hall and wait,' said Badger. 'Perhaps Toad will come back – and perhaps he won't.'

At lunchtime, Toad was a long way from Toad Hall. He came to a small town. He felt very hungry.

Then he saw a café across the road. Its name was *The Black Horse*. He went inside and had some lunch.

Suddenly, he heard a noise outside: '*Poop! Poop!*' He remembered that noise very well. It was a car!

The driver of the car came into *The Black Horse* for lunch. Toad finished his food and went outside. He looked at the car.

It was a beautiful new car! Toad looked at it for a long time. He was very excited. It was wonderful! He opened the door and got in.

'I want the doctor, Ratty. Can you bring him to me, please?'

'Does this car start easily?' he thought. He started it and drove away. He didn't think. He only wanted to be in the car. 'It's a good life!' he cried happily.

But the police caught Toad. Next day, he had to go in front of the judge. The judge was very angry with him.

'Toad,' he said. 'You are a very bad animal. You took that car and you drove it very dangerously. So now you have to go to prison for twenty years.'

Chapter 7   Toad's Adventures

When Toad arrived in the dark, cold prison, he cried. Twenty years is a very long time.

'This is the end of Toad. The end of everything! My dear friends won't remember me. Why didn't I listen to Badger and Ratty and Mole? They were right and I was wrong.'

But life in prison wasn't very bad. One of the prison officers had a pretty daughter. This girl liked animals and she felt very sad for Toad. One day she said to her father, 'Please can I talk to Toad? He looks ill and unhappy. I want to take him some good food.'

'Yes, you can see him,' said her father.

The girl took Toad some tea, some bread and a cake. Then she talked to him and asked him questions. Toad began to feel better. He told her about Toad Hall and his life there.

After that, the girl visited Toad every day. She always took food for him.

'Toad was wrong when he took that car,' she thought. 'But he's sad about it now. I have to help him.'

When she saw Toad again, she said, 'Toad, listen. I have an idea. My aunt is a washerwoman. She washes clothes for the people in the prison. She takes the dirty clothes from the prison every

Monday. Then she washes them and brings them back every Friday. You're very rich, Toad. Give my aunt some money and she'll give you her clothes. Then you can leave the prison and nobody will know you.'

Toad didn't want to wear a washerwoman's clothes. But he didn't want to stay in prison for twenty years. So he thought about it, and then he said, 'That's a very good idea.'

The next afternoon, the girl came into Toad's room with her aunt. Toad gave the washerwoman twenty pounds and she gave him her clothes. So he left the prison. But now he had another problem – he didn't know the way home. Then he heard a train. 'Aha!' he cried. 'That's the answer!'

But Toad couldn't get on the train because he had no money. He began to cry. The train arrived and the driver saw him. The driver said, 'Hello, washerwoman! Why are you sad?'

'I haven't got any money,' cried Toad. 'I have to get home tonight, or my children will have no food.'

'Don't cry,' said the driver kindly. 'You don't have to pay anything. Jump up here and sit with me.'

So Toad jumped up on to the train. He felt very happy. He was on his way home now. After some time, the driver suddenly said, 'Something's wrong. There's another train behind us. It's going very fast too. There are a lot of policemen on it.'

Then Toad had to tell the driver everything. 'Help me! Help me!' he said. 'Dear Mr Driver, I'm not a washerwoman and I haven't got any children. I'm Mr Toad of Toad Hall. I ran away from prison. The policemen will catch me and send me back there for twenty years.'

'But why were you in prison?' asked the driver.

'I only took a car,' said Toad. 'I didn't think. I was very bad but I won't do it again.'

'I'll help you,' said the driver. 'Listen, Toad. We're coming to a long dark tunnel. At the other end of the tunnel, there's a wood.

'Something's wrong. There's another train behind us.'

I'll go very slowly there and you can jump off the train. The other train will be in the tunnel and the police won't see you.'

'Thank you! Thank you!' cried Toad.

The train went through the tunnel and Toad jumped off. He ran quickly into the wood. Two minutes later, he saw the police train. It didn't stop. Toad laughed and laughed.

But it was late and he was very cold and hungry. He was also afraid – the wood was very quiet and dark. He found a hole under a tree and climbed into it. Then he tried to sleep.

Chapter 8　More Adventures

The next morning, Toad woke up very early because he was very cold. He started to walk, but he didn't know the way to Toad Hall. After some time, he came to a river. There was a boat on the river with a woman on it. A horse walked on the river bank in front of the boat and pulled it.

'Good morning,' the woman called to Toad.

'It's not a very good morning for me,' answered Toad. 'I'm a washerwoman but I had to leave my job. My daughter wants my help, and I'm trying to go to her. But I don't know the way and I haven't got any money. She lives near the river – near a fine house. The name of the house is Toad Hall. Do you know it?'

'Yes, of course,' the woman said. 'And I'm going very near there. Get in the boat and I'll take you.'

'Oh, thank you, thank you,' said Toad and got in. After some minutes, the boatwoman said, 'So you're a washerwoman? Can you help me? I have a lot of dirty clothes, but I can't wash them. I haven't got time. Will you wash the clothes for me?'

'Er...er...er...' began Toad. Then he thought, 'Everybody can wash clothes. It's easy.' So he said, 'Yes, I'll wash them for you.'

So he tried to wash the dirty clothes. But it wasn't easy. He tried for nearly an hour, but the clothes weren't clean. Then suddenly the woman said, 'You aren't a washerwoman. You can't wash clothes.' She began to laugh at him. Toad was very angry.

'Of course I'm not a washerwoman. I'm Mr Toad of Toad Hall, he said.'

'Ugh!' said the woman. 'A dirty toad on my boat. Get out!' And she took Toad's leg and threw him into the river.

Toad was very, very angry now. The water was cold and his clothes were heavy. But he got to the river bank. Then he saw the boatwoman's horse and jumped on its back. The horse ran away with Toad on it.

'Stop! Stop!' shouted the boatwoman.

But Toad didn't stop. He came to a road and saw a caravan in front of him. Outside the caravan, a man sat by a fire and cooked some food.

Toad was very hungry. But he couldn't ask the man for food because he didn't have any money.

Then the man said to Toad, 'Do you want to sell that horse?'

Toad was very surprised and happy. He sold the horse to the man. Then the man gave him some breakfast too. The food was very good.

Toad started to walk to Toad Hall. He was very happy. He walked, and he sang a little song. 'I'm a clever Toad,' he thought. 'I got out of prison and the police couldn't catch me. And now I have some money too.'

Toad walked for about an hour, then he began to feel tired. He heard a car behind him. 'I'll talk to the driver. Perhaps he'll take me to Toad Hall,' he thought. The car stopped and Toad looked at it again. Suddenly he didn't feel happy.

'Oh, no,' he thought. 'That car was outside *The Black Horse*. I took it – it's the same car. And it's the same driver! He'll take me to the police and I'll be in prison again!'

Then he saw the boatwoman's horse and jumped on its back.

Toad sat down on the road and closed his eyes. The driver got out of the car. He was with a friend.

'This washerwoman looks very ill,' the men said. 'Let's take her to the next village. Perhaps she has friends there.'

The two men were very kind to Toad. They put him in the front of the car and the driver started it. Toad opened his eyes. He was in a car again!

'Are you feeling better now?' asked the driver.

'Yes, thank you,' said Toad. For a time, he didn't say anything, then he asked, 'Please, sir, can I drive the car? Only for a little way.'

The driver laughed and the other man said, 'The road is very quiet. Yes, you can drive.'

And so Toad drove the car. He drove carefully for a minute or two, but then he drove very fast. The men shouted at him, 'Be careful, washerwoman!' But Toad didn't listen.

'This is wonderful!' he shouted. 'But I'm not really a washerwoman. I'm clever Mr Toad. The best driver in the world. You can't stop me now!'

'Toad – *the* Toad!' cried the two men. 'You took our car! Stop, stop! We'll take you to the police.'

But Toad didn't stop. He drove very, very fast. The car went off the road and hit a tree. Toad jumped out and ran away. The doors of the car were broken and the two men had to climb out. They ran after Toad.

Toad ran and ran. Then he looked behind him. The two men were near him now. Suddenly he fell into some water. It was the river. Toad tried to swim, but he was too tired.

Then a hand pushed him to the bank, and somebody said, 'Good morning, Toad. What are you doing here?'

It was Ratty.

Chapter 9 Toad Sees his Friends Again

Rat pushed Toad out of the water and into his hole.

'Oh, Rat,' said Toad. 'Thank you. I'm having a lot of adventures. I'll tell you about them.'

'Wait a minute, Toad,' said Rat. 'Go and take off those wet clothes. Why are you wearing a washerwoman's clothes? You look very stupid. Go and change your clothes.'

When Toad was in dry clothes, lunch was on the table. They ate, and Toad told Rat about his adventures.

'I'm very clever, Ratty,' he said again and again. 'I got out of prison. The police followed me but I got away. I took a horse and sold it. I got a lot of money. Then I drove a car very fast. I'm very clever.'

Rat was quiet for a long time. Then he said, 'I don't want to hurt you, Toad. But you're not clever. You took a car and went to prison. Does that mean nothing to you? And didn't you think about Mole and Badger and me? People say bad things about us because we're your friends.'

'Oh, Ratty!' cried Toad. 'From today, I'm going to be good. I'm not interested in cars now. Cars are boring. Let's go to Toad Hall. I want to see it again.'

'Go to Toad Hall?' cried Rat. 'But Toad, we can't go there. The weasels are living in Toad Hall now.'

'What!' said Toad. He began to cry. Then he said, 'What happened, Ratty? Please tell me everything.'

'Well,' said Rat. 'When you went to prison ... When you went away, Badger and Mole stayed at Toad Hall. Then one cold, dark night, the weasels from the Wild Wood went there. They had guns and knives and sticks. They threw Badger and Mole out of the house.'

'Now the weasels live there. They're eating your food, and drinking your drink. They're sleeping in your beds. The place is very dirty, and a lot of things are broken. It's very sad, Toad.'

'My beautiful Toad Hall,' cried Toad. 'What am I going to do? I want to go there now. I want to fight those weasels.'

'But you can't,' said Rat. 'There are a lot of them. We tried to get into the house, but they have guns. Listen, Toad. Badger and Mole are coming here this afternoon. Perhaps they'll have some new ideas.'

'Oh, good,' said Toad. 'How are Badger and Mole? I didn't ask you about them.'

'Why didn't you ask, Toad?' Rat said. 'Badger and Mole are your very good friends. They watch Toad Hall carefully and they know everything about the weasels.'

'Oh, Rat,' said Toad. 'I forgot Badger and Mole. I'm a bad Toad.'

Later, Badger and Mole came. They were very surprised when they saw Toad. Mole said, 'Good afternoon, Toad. This is nice. But how did you get out of prison? You are clever!'

'Don't ask him any questions, Mole,' said Rat. 'He isn't clever. He's very stupid. Now let's sit down and have some tea. Did you go to Toad Hall today? How are things there?'

After the four animals finished tea, Mole said, 'We can't find a way into Toad Hall. There are weasels outside with guns. When they see us, they laugh.'

Then Badger said, 'We can't fight the weasels outside. There are a lot of them and there are only four of us. But there is another way. Listen. I'm going to tell you something very important. There's a tunnel under the ground. It goes from the river bank into the middle of Toad Hall.'

'But there isn't a tunnel,' Toad laughed. 'I know Toad Hall very well and I don't know anything about a tunnel.'

'I'm telling you ... there *is* a tunnel,' said Badger. 'Toad's father told me about it. Only I know about it. Now ... there's going to be a big party at Toad Hall tomorrow night. This is my plan. Tomorrow night we'll go through the tunnel and come up inside the house. The tunnel comes out in the room next to the party. When they see us, the weasels will be very surprised. And they won't have guns at the party. Only the weasels outside the house will have guns.

'Without their guns and sticks, the weasels aren't very brave. So we can fight them and win easily.'

'That's a good plan, Badger!' cried Rat, Mole and Toad.

Toad slept very well that night. He got up late the next morning and went downstairs. Mole was out. Rat was very busy. On the table there were a lot of of guns, sticks and knives.

'A gun for Badger. A gun for Mole. A gun for Toad, and a gun for me,' Rat said quietly. 'A stick for Badger. A stick for Mole. A stick for Toad, and a stick for me.'

'Ratty,' said Badger. 'Why do we want these guns and knives and things? Let's only take sticks.'

'Perhaps we'll want the guns and knives too,' said Rat.

After lunch, the other three animals waited for Mole. Where was he? Was there a problem?

Chapter 10   The Fight for Toad Hall

Late in the afternoon, Mole came in. He looked very excited.

'I went to Toad Hall,' he cried. 'I had a wonderful time.'

'Tell us about it,' said Toad.

'I found Toad's washerwoman's clothes this morning,' he said, 'and I had an idea. I put on the clothes and went to Toad Hall. I talked to the weasels outside the Hall. Then a big weasel came out of the house.

'"Go away, washerwoman!" he said. "We don't want you here." "Go away?" I said. "You weasels will have to go away, not me. I work for Mr Badger and I'll tell you something. A hundred brave, strong badgers are coming to Toad Hall with hundreds of rats and toads and moles. They're going to fight you and throw you out." The weasels were very afraid.'

'Good, Mole,' said Badger. 'That's very clever.'

Toad didn't understand. 'Why is that clever?' he thought.

When it was dark, they met at Rat's front door. Rat gave each animal a gun, a stick and a knife. Then Badger took a light and said, 'Follow me!' They walked by the river bank for a little way. Badger was in front, then Rat, then Mole, and then Toad. Then Badger went into a hole in the bank. Mole and Rat followed him easily, but Toad fell into the river. Mole and Rat pulled him out – he was very wet and cold. Badger was very angry. He said, 'One more stupid thing, Toad, and we'll go without you.'

It was cold and dark and wet inside the tunnel. Toad couldn't walk very fast.

'Quickly, Toad!' shouted Rat.

After a long time, they heard a noise above their heads.

'The weasels are having a good party,' said Badger. 'Good! They won't hear us.'

The tunnel began to go up. They came out of the tunnel through a door in the floor. They were in the room next to the party! There was a lot of noise.

'Follow me!' cried Badger. He opened the door and the four friends ran into the middle of the party. They used their guns and sticks and knives. Some weasels fell to the floor. Other weasels hit their heads on the table.

The four friends ran everywhere and fought very bravely. The weasels were surprised and afraid. Then they remembered the words of the washerwoman.

'There are hundreds of moles, rats, badgers and toads here,' they thought. Then Toad hit the most important weasel very hard and he fell down on the floor. Now the fight was at an end. The other weasels ran away. Badger was right. Without their guns and sticks, the weasels weren't very brave.

'You have your house again, Toad,' said Badger.

'Thank you,' said Toad. 'Thank you very much.'

The four friends ran everywhere and fought very bravely.

The four animals found a lot of food in the dining-room. They were very hungry, so they ate it. Then Badger asked, 'Where are we going to sleep? Mole and Toad, go and look at the beds.'

Toad wasn't happy. This was his house, not Badger's! But he didn't say anything. He went with Mole, and ten minutes later they came back again.

'There are four clean beds,' said Mole. 'But the house is very dirty and a lot of things are broken. We'll have a lot of work tomorrow.'

'We'll think about that in the morning,' said Badger. 'Now let's go to bed.'

Chapter 11   Toad's Big Party

When Toad came downstairs the next morning, it was very late. Mole and Rat were in the garden in the sun. Badger was inside. He looked up when Toad came into the room.

'Good morning, Toad,' he said. 'So here you are! I want to talk to you about your party.'

Toad was very surprised.

'Party? What party?' he asked.

'The party for your friends,' Badger said. 'You're home again now. You have to have a big party.'

'Oh,' said Toad. 'Yes, of course. When shall we have the party? Next Saturday?'

'No, tonight,' Badger said.

'Oh,' said Toad. 'I haven't got much time.'

'No,' said Badger. 'So you'll have to write the invitations now. Here's some paper and a pen. I want you to ask your friends to the party.'

'But, Badger,' said Toad. 'I'm very hungry. Can I have some

breakfast? And then I want to go and look at my house and garden. It's a beautiful day. I don't want to stay inside and write invitations – not today, please.'

Badger began to look angry, so Toad said quickly, 'Of course I'll write the invitations now, Badger. You're always right. I can look at my garden later.'

'Good, Toad,' said Badger, and he left the room. Toad went to his desk. Then he had an idea – and he started to laugh.

'I'll write the invitations,' he thought. 'Then tonight I'll tell everybody about me – the brave and clever Toad. I really am the cleverest Toad in the world. And I'll write some songs and sing them at the party too.' Toad felt very happy.

He sat down and began to write. He worked all morning.

—— INVITATION ——

Please come to a party
tonight at Toad Hall.
Toad will make three
speeches about his
adventures and he will
sing some songs.

After Toad finished the invitations, he gave them to the postman. 'Take these invitations to my friends,' he said. 'And be quick! We haven't much time.'

The four animals met for lunch at one o'clock. Nobody talked very much, but after lunch Badger said, 'Come with me, Toad. I want to talk to you. We'll go into the other room. Come with us, Rat.'

Inside the room, Badger said, 'We saw your stupid invitations, Toad. We stopped the postman before lunch. You'll have to write

So Toad sang his last song.

some new invitations. We don't want any songs at the party tonight. And your friends know the story of your adventures, so you don't have to tell them again.'

'Please understand, Toad,' said Rat. 'Your friends like you very much, but you have to stop talking about your house, your garden and your adventures.'

'You're right, Ratty,' Toad said sadly. 'I'll try to change. I'll try — really. And now I'll go and write some new invitations.' And he left the room.

'Oh, Badger,' cried Rat. 'I hate being unkind to Toad.'

'I hate it too,' said Badger. 'But we're his friends. We have to tell him these things.'

Evening came, and Toad's friends arrived at Toad Hall for the party. Toad was in his bedroom. He felt a little sad.

'My friends are right,' he thought. 'I have to change — I know that. But first, I'm going to sing one last song. But I won't sing it at the party. I'll sing it here in my bedroom.'

So Toad sang his last song. Then he went down and met his friends. The party was wonderful. Everybody was very happy because Toad was at Toad Hall again. Then Otter asked Toad about his adventures. 'Tell us everything, Toad!'

'No, no, I really can't, my friends,' Toad said.

Toad was different now!

◆

After the big party, the four friends started their old way of life again. Badger went back to his house in the Wild Wood. Rat and Mole went to Rat's house by the river. Toad lived quietly at Toad Hall. He sent some money to the prison officer's daughter. He wrote a nice letter to the train driver. He bought a new horse for the boatwoman. And he didn't buy any more cars!

ACTIVITIES

Chapters 1–4

Before you read

1 Look at the picture of animals opposite page 1. Do you have these animals in your country? What do you know about them? Where do they live?

2 Find these words in your dictionary. They are all in the story.
   bank broken caravan dust Hall hole row (v) surprised stick tunnel wild willow
   Which is a word for:
   a a kind of tree?
   b a home for a small animal?
   c a large house in the country?
   d a long, dark place?
   e a place next to a river?
   What are the other words in your language?

After you read

3 Which of these five animals in the story – Rat, Mole, Otter, Toad and Badger:
   a lives under the ground?
   b is a very good swimmer?
   c sleeps for many hours each day in the winter?
   d lives in the Wild Wood?
   e is always interested in new things?
   f has a boat?

4 Answer these questions:
   a Why doesn't Rat want to visit Badger?
   b Why isn't Toad angry about his broken caravan?
   c What makes Mole afraid in the Wild Wood?

Chapters 5–8

Before you read

5 How will Badger help Rat and Mole?

6 Find these words in your dictionary.

adventure   judge   lock   officer   prison   washerwoman

   a Which words are for people?

   b Which word is for a place?

   c What do you do to a door?

   d Which word means something exciting?

After you read

7 Work with a friend.

   Student A: You are Rat. Toad is not at Toad Hall. How did he get away? Tell Badger.

   Student B: You are Badger. Listen to Rat and ask questions. You are very angry.

8 How do these people help Toad?

   a the pretty girl   **b** the train driver

   c the boatwoman   **d** the man with the caravan

Chapters 9–11

Before you read

9 What problems will Toad have now? What do you think?

10 Find these words in your dictionary. Use each word in a sentence.

   brave   invitation

After you read

11 Who says these things? Who are they talking to?

   a 'I hate being unkind to Toad.'

   b 'But there isn't a tunnel.'

   c 'We'll have a lot of work tomorrow.'

   d 'You have to have a big party.'

12 Work with a friend.

   Student A: You are Otter at Toad's party. Ask Toad about his adventures. You really want to hear about them. What do you say to him?

   Student B: You are Toad. Listen to Otter and answer his questions.

Writing

13 You are Toad. After Badger and Rat talk to you, write a new party invitation for your friends.

14 You are Toad, and you are at Toad Hall at the end of the story. Write a letter to the train driver *or* to the prison officer's daughter.

15 Tell the story of the fight for Toad Hall.

16 Rat and Mole are good friends. How are they different? Why are they friends?